AF365364

...AND WHY NOT?

A step closer to living a more fulfilling life

Sophie Burrus - Müller

First published in 2023
© Sophie Burrus - Müller
...And Why Not?, Sophie Burrus - Müller

ISBN print 978-2-9701706-1-7
ISBN e-book 978-2-9701706-0-0

All rights reserved. No part of this book may be reproduced, scanned, stored in a retrieval system, or distributed in any form including printed or electronic without prior written permission from the author. Please do not participate in or encourage piracy of copyrighted materials.

Created in conjunction with The Book Shelf Ltd.

Although the author has made every effort to ensure that the information in this book was correct at the time of publishing, and while this publication is designed to provide accurate information on the subject matter covered, the author assumes no responsibility for errors, inaccuracies, omissions, or any other inconsistencies herein, and hereby disclaims any liability to any party for any loss, damage, or disruption caused by errors or omissions, whether such errors or omissions result from negligence, accident, or any other cause. The author makes no guarantees concerning the level of success you may experience by following the advice contained in this book, and you accept the risk that results will differ for each individual.

You can find my artwork at the website below.

www.sm-artpaintings.com

CONTENTS

DEDICATION

To my family, more specifically my parents and my dear husband, for believing in me and being so supportive of my projects.

Writing a book and sharing a message that can help and perhaps bring comfort to people has always been a dream of mine and here I am, finally realizing it.

INTRODUCTION

Hello! If you are reading these lines, it's probably for a reason. Either you came across this book while browsing and the title caught your attention, or you heard about it from a friend, or someone gifted it to you…

Whatever the reason, I am thrilled that someone has picked up this book! Hopefully, in the next few lines, I will capture your attention and motivate you to continue reading the next few pages.

Here I am, pounding away at my keyboard, just 6 weeks away from my due date to deliver my first child. I had an epiphany at 4 AM last night that "…And Why Not?" would be the topic I attempted to write a book about.

The aim would be to share my words of wisdom on what I have experienced so far in my life, and hopefully this will help you or someone you know who has experienced or is currently experiencing a similar situation.

What situation am I talking about, you might wonder? Well,

I mean the situation that we all go through in life at some point—some more subtly than others, but we all go through it. One day, we wake up or something happens in our life that makes us realize something needs to change. We notice that there is something deep down inside of us, what we often describe as a "gut feeling," that says we need to do things differently or try something new.

Do you have that feeling now? Or have you faced this feeling before?

Are you among the lucky ones who know what needs to change but have no clue where this path will take you?

Or do you know where this change will take you but don't know what the next step should be?

You're probably wondering: Is this the right change to make? Am I on the right path? Is this the right thing to do? Will it turn out for the best?

Yes, I know this can be nerve-wracking and frustrating, and it can often lead us to the decision not to make any changes purely out of fear. This is the famous fear of the unknown. However, I have learned and live from the philosophy that if you don't try, you can never know.

So, you want to make a change or try something new in life ... And Why Not?

Of course, I'm not telling you to live your life recklessly and put your hand on a hot stove because you feel like testing it. You know that your hand will get burned, and you are probably better off avoiding unnecessary pain and keeping both hands healthy. So, it's important that you weigh up the pros and cons of the decision you are about to make. I'm probably not teaching you anything new here, but there is no escaping from this one… all of your decisions and choices have consequences. It's up to you to decide whether more gain or pain will come from what you're about to undertake.

The decision is yours, and you are the only one who can take it and put it into action. You and only you can bring change to your life. Only you can make you live the life that you want and need. Why do I insist on this point? Because we often tend to forget that we alone are the main actor in our life story—the protagonist—and only we have the power to take the plot where we want to take it.

We all have our own journey to live on this planet and our own lessons to learn. Some have it easier than others because they are content with the way they have lived or are currently living their life and do not see the need to make a change. Others are faced with situations that give them no choice but to make a change if they want to survive. Some people, like me, wake up one morning and realize there is more to life, and even though things are good and changing things would probably seem crazy to others, we feel deep down that it is the right thing to do.

I am an avid believer that there is no worse thing in life than living with regrets. If you have the opportunity to do something differently or try something new because your gut, intuition, or something inside you tells you it is the right thing to do, then go for it! There will always be a million reasons that you can come up with not to do it. Or there will be people in your entourage who tell you why you should not change because they want to protect you or think they know what is best for you. But if it feels right to you, even though you might think you are taking a leap of faith, ask yourself "… And Why Not?"

So, let's start this adventure together. My intention in this book is to use my own experience to bring you words and colors of comfort and perhaps guidance that will hopefully help you take a step, make a decision, find the courage, embrace your life journey, and put in place the changes you need to make to live a more fulfilling life.

You will notice that before each chapter, there is a painting or illustration. One of my other passions is painting, and it is a way of expressing myself, just like I am doing in words through these pages. For me, writing this book is opening up to the world, and if painting was not part of this book, it would be like sharing only half of who I am. This is my way of expressing the subject of the chapter with colors. I hope you enjoy it and find your own color in life.

At the end of each chapter, you will notice a Personal Notes & Reflections section. This is for you to write down your own thoughts to help you reflect on your process.

So, let's begin.

Chapter 1

LISTEN AND WATCH OUT
FOR SIGNS

As humans, we are people of habit, and very often we find ourselves caught up in a routine, which means we become less alert or aware of the signs around us. Sometimes, we go so far down a path that we only realize something is off and we need to change after we get a wake-up call.

The point I am making here is that even if you are in a comfortable and well-established routine and don't feel the need to make any changes, you should still try every now and then to take a step back and do a quick check.

As you have probably heard, change is the only constant in life. Some changes are more subtle than others, and often we end up making these small changes without noticing as we go with the flow of life. Other times, things get a bit more intense if we decide to resist the change and navigate against the current.

Either way, change will knock on our door at some point in our life, and if we stay alert and listen carefully, then we can quickly pick up on these sometimes subtle signs—the things that tell us it's time to do something different. And if we ignore these signs, they will only intensify until we get the message.

So, doing a bit of introspection every now and then doesn't hurt. Ask yourself: Is my body telling me something? For instance, do you often not feel well, or do you notice that you're getting sick fairly often? Many people will say "Ah, it's just flu season and everyone is sick." Sure, but if you're generally not someone who gets sick often, you might want to ask yourself: "What am I doing or not doing that is causing this?" or "Is there something I should change?" Why wait until you need to be hospitalized or have a breakdown that puts you in a situation where you have no choice?

This doesn't just happen with the negative—we can also find the same in positive experiences. Perhaps you have a well-established, comfortable routine and suddenly go to an art expo that takes you back to childhood when you used to paint. You don't know where from, but the experience gives you butterflies in your stomach. You come out of the expo and go on with your life, then suddenly you start seeing articles about art and meet people who paint for a hobby… is life perhaps trying to tell you something here? These are the signs I'm talking about! If you are alert, you might pick up on these signs earlier and decide to start painting again, only to realize a few years down the line that not only does it bring balance into your life, but this change led you to meet people and get opportunities to thrive doing what you love!

The alternative is that you can choose to ignore the signs and tell yourself "I don't have time for this," and perhaps let an opportunity go by that could have brought you a greater sense of fulfillment in life.

There is no right or wrong choice here. All I'm saying is that life puts opportunities in front of us more often than we think, and if we are awake and alert, we can make the necessary changes and seize these chances.

What do I mean by this? Well, I don't know what your belief system is, and we are definitely not here to discuss that. Whether you believe in God, Buddha, the Powers Above, the Universe, or nothing at all, I am not here to judge you, and it is your right to believe in what you want. What I do believe is that we have each come to Earth to fulfill a specific mission. Sometimes we get a bit lost on our path, and life will always offer signs and opportunities to put us back on track. If we stay attentive, we can pick up on these signs and make the required adjustments. Or we can simply choose to ignore what comes our way and perhaps live a good life but not fulfill what we truly came to Earth for.

We often reach a fork in the road of our life journey where we have to pick whether to go left or right. There is no right or wrong choice, but we do have to make a choice. Sometimes, this decision will take us away from our purpose for a while until life finds a way to give us another opportunity to get back on track. But if you choose to ignore the signs, it's a choice like any other and there is nothing wrong with that. You are perhaps just letting the opportunity to live a more fulfilling life go by.

I had this experience not so long ago where I could choose to continue a very successful and promising corporate career or make a shift to focus on what matters the most deep inside me: my family and developing my true potential as an artist and entrepreneur. Not to mention the other hidden talents that I might discover down the road.

It took me some time to realize I was at that fork in the road, and I must say it was not an easy decision to make. Not from a family point of view, but more from the perspective of leaving a career that had brought a certain stability to realize my dreams. At that stage, they were dreams or ideas I had put to the side, like we often do, because they were things that I hadn't found the time to really work on, telling myself "One day, when I'm older, perhaps I will materialize them."

Well, it seems that life had different plans for me in terms of timing! Now that I think back, there were signs along the way. Often, in conversations with my parents or people I met, they said that I had great potential to do whatever I set my mind to and that I should enjoy my life more. Yet I was so busy in my work life that I often thought "That's great encouragement and I'll keep it in mind for later when I have time to work on these dreams and projects." Of course, I never found that time… that is, until one day when I was on vacation and had the opportunity to disconnect from work. Suddenly, this feeling inside me woke up and said "It's time to make a change!"

I assume you can guess which direction I took? In fact, writing a book was one of the projects I told myself that one day I would realize, and here we are!

Was it easy to make this change? No. Do I have any regrets? Not at all! I'm thankful that I was able to pick up on the signs and follow my gut… because this new direction brought me so many blessings that would probably never have occurred if I had taken the other path, and the other path may have led me to situations that I would regret today, like not getting to spend time with my family.

Even though there is no regret in choosing a new path, it's

worth noting that when you unplug from a routine that has previously consumed most of your day, the beginning will not necessarily be a smooth ride.

In my case, there I was—at home, with so many projects in mind—and I wondered where on earth to start?

You might ask "Well, why didn't you just start working on your projects in parallel instead of leaving your job, then make the change when everything was planned and you were ready to roll?" But like a good old friend of mine often says "If you want to make God laugh, make a plan."

Could I have tried to do this? Yes.

Would I have succeeded? Probably not, because I was so caught up in my work and other things that I actually didn't have the inspiration to paint or think about my book, nor did I really have the energy to start building a business plan.

What is more, not trying to do both at once had an unexpected benefit. While I tried to figure out where to start, I had the incredible opportunity to spend quality time with my grandmother, who lived to 102, in the last year of her life. I also had time to spend quality moments with my parents, with my husband, and with my friends. I got to meet great people who I would probably never have crossed paths with if I had carried on my career path—people I have since collaborated with on various projects.

As I embarked on this new journey, my inspiration (which was well hidden in the back of a drawer) started coming back. I began painting again, which opened up an amazing opportunity to get involved in a start-up that helps farmers finance their transition to regenerative agriculture through my art!

I met amazing people who, through their challenges and advice, helped me put a plan on paper for my lifelong boutique hotel retreat dream.

And I am finally writing this book!

Above all, I am blessed and honored to say that after writing this book, I welcomed the most precious gift in life, my little bundle of joy, as a first-time mom!

Am I at the end of this journey and have I achieved everything I wanted to? No.

Have I figured everything out? Definitely not!

But what I can say is if I had not picked up on the signs and had continued on my career path, I probably would have missed out on a great deal of things that I got the opportunity to live on the new path, and what a shame it would have been.

What I want to conclude this chapter with is… listen and watch out for the signs. Life has a lot of wonderful surprises out there for you. Seize the opportunities when they come. And if you are afraid of making a change, ask yourself "… And Why Not?"

Thoughts & Reflections

Chapter 2

THE ONLY EXPERT ON YOURSELF IS YOU

Like the world-renowned Mexican artist Frida Kahlo, who used to paint self-portraits with the justification that she was the subject she knew best, this is also true for each one of us. The only expert on yourself is you.

Yes, perhaps your parents or people you grew up with tell you that they know you, and they probably do. At least better than people you have only just met or have a purely professional relationship with. But the only person who can really tell how you feel, what you are experiencing, and what is going on inside your head, ultimately, is you.

Sometimes, it's not easy to put a finger on what we are feeling—and we tend to speak to others to help us figure it out, or at least put a name to what we're going through. Sometimes this helps, but other times it doesn't because other people can only see from the outside or they can only see the tip of the iceberg. So they may tell you "You seem angry," and then you tell yourself "Then I must be angry." But is it really anger you are feeling? Or is it just a symptom of something else? This you can only answer yourself by asking the right questions.

This is an exercise that often requires a bit of introspection and a lot of the famous question "Why?"

"Why am I feeling angry?" Perhaps because you feel frustrated?

"Why am I feeling frustrated?" Perhaps because you feel you are not in control of the situation?

"Why I am feeling not in control?" Maybe because you fear something?

"What is it that I fear?" Well, that one, only you can answer.

I think you get the point, and I am not saying this is the absolute sequence to follow, but it does help. It often takes courage to sit down and take time to go through this exercise as you don't know what you'll find out. But trust me, it is worth it.

At the end of this exercise, if you are able to, take time to understand what is putting you in this state or making you feel this way. Doing so will not solve your problem, but it will give you the clarity to navigate through it and perhaps be more understanding toward yourself and others.

As humans, we experience a lot of emotions, which all too often we let take over, and BOOM, here comes the rollercoaster ride! You are so taken over by the feeling or sensation that you cannot think of anything else. You cannot hear or sense anything other than the emotion you are experiencing.

It's okay to feel angry or happy or sad, and it's okay to be aware of it and acknowledge it. However, try not to get stuck in it for too long as you'll miss out on what's happening around you, which might have other consequences.

Easier said than done, yes. But what I am trying to say here is that if you feel ecstatic and happy because you've received some great news, fantastic! Still, you need to come down from your cloud enough to be mindful of your surroundings as you might act insensitively toward someone or cross the road without looking or have some kind of accident while in your happy bubble.

This passage on emotions might seem like we've gone off on a sidetrack, but it isn't really. Emotions are part of us, and we have to live with them. And going back to my point from the beginning of this chapter, how and what you feel, only you can really know.

I am not telling you to overanalyze everything and spend hours trying to figure out how you feel about every little thing that happens in your life. I am saying that every now and then, it won't harm you to introspect, especially if you are at a tipping point in your life where you have to make a decision. Otherwise, you become like a little kid covering their ears and screaming "Lalala, I can't hear you!" The reality is still going on; you're just not listening to it.

Are you feeling angry or frustrated? Do you fear a certain situation? If so, so what? You have the right to feel the way you feel, and it is only through figuring out what makes you feel this way that you will gain the clarity to make a conscious decision.

In other words, follow your gut feeling. What is your gut telling you to do? You are the only one who knows the answer. And how do you listen to your gut? Well, by understanding the true cause of what you are feeling.

Only then will you be able to distinguish between what your gut feeling is truly telling you versus what your emotions are covering up.

If your gut feeling is guiding you, but you are still having doubts because you aren't sure where the path will take you, ask yourself "… And Why Not?"

Thoughts & Reflections

Chapter 3

WILL THIS MAKE
YOU HAPPY?

When you're considering making a change, you might wonder, "Will this change I am about to make in my life bring me happiness?" Honestly, I don't know, and I can't answer that. If you have weighed up the pros and cons of your decision, then you should get a sense of the answer to this question. However, as I said earlier, it is sometimes the case that when you decide on the change, you might not feel all that great about it at the beginning. Especially when your emotions get in the way and you start going over the decision you have taken or the change you have made, and your mind starts spinning like a wheel, then you start to doubt whether you made the right choice at all.

Let me try to bring you some comfort in all of this… if the decision or change you have initiated came from your gut because deep inside you, it felt right, then don't doubt your decision. Some people might instantly feel that a weight has been lifted off their shoulders, but for others, it will take time, and it might take you some time. Trust me, with the passage of time, you will one day look back and tell yourself "I made the right decision."

I believe that if the change comes from your gut or intuition, it's for the best. Sometimes, what is best is not what we think it will turn out to be, but it's still the right thing to do. This change will trigger other changes or bring other opportunities into your life, and at some point (maybe a few years down the line), you'll look back and have the reflection "Well, if I hadn't done this, I would never have ended up here today."

You might be wondering… where is happiness in all of this? All of us want to be happy. That's why one of the most common scenes in life is a parent telling their child "All I want for you is to be happy." I would ask, what even is happiness? Who defines it? Is my definition of happiness the same as yours? Probably not. A piece of chocolate might make me happy, while for you, happiness might be buying flowers or going for a run…

Happiness is:
1) subjective, and
2) what you decide to make out of the situation.

Happiness, like a very wise man once told me, is a state of mind. And if you think about it, this makes sense.

But just in case, let me give you an example of this.

I was once involved in a verbally abusive relationship (though thankfully not physically abusive). At the time, I was young and didn't really realize what was going on, or at least I didn't want to see it. Every negative event was followed by a shower of gifts and apologies, so I told myself "My partner has a strong character, but deep inside, he is good as he realizes when he has done something wrong and apologizes."

Yes, this is perhaps a typical cliché, and I will confirm that when you are caught up in the game, it's hard to tell what is going on. Looking at the situation today, I would never let something like this happen again and let anyone talk to me that way. But back in the day, when I was young and inexperienced, I told myself "This must be normal."

One day, a situation occurred where he accused me of something I hadn't done. It was such an unfair situation that suddenly, a feeling deep inside me surged so strongly that I found myself standing up to the situation, and with a very assertive and directive voice, I said "Enough! Don't you ever speak to me like that again!" It was as though it was my soul speaking out, and thank God it did!

You can guess what happened next… the following day, he said that we should maybe take a break. The relationship came to an end fairly quickly.

Was I happy? No.

It took me several months of putting myself in doubt over whether I had done the right thing, right down to the point of telling myself that I was not worthy of being loved. Drama, drama, oh… what emotions and your ego can drive you to think of yourself sometimes!

At the time, I was thankfully surrounded by a great support system, but it still took a lot of alone time and self-reflection to forgive myself, accept the situation, and move forward. It took me some time to heal, and I didn't engage in a serious relationship until a few years later.

Do I regret the decision and change I made at the time? Not

a single bit! Because thanks to that change, I had the chance to seize different opportunities that led me to where I am today, which I would probably have never come across if I had stayed in my old patterns.

Am I happy with my life? That again is a matter of perspective and how we, or in this case I, want to see things. But in this particular case, I can say that this change brought happiness into my life in the end. We can make something mediocre out of what would be considered a very positive and privileged situation if we tend to see the glass as half-empty. Or vice versa.

Let's take the example of two children getting ice cream. Robert wanted chocolate but there was only strawberry available, so he got his ice cream but wasn't content as he didn't get exactly what he wanted. John would have preferred chocolate ice cream and got strawberry but was delighted anyway because he got a refreshing treat on a hot summer's day. It's all about perspective.

So, to go back to the question… am I happy with my current life? In simple terms, yes. But I prefer to see it from the point of view of gratefulness and fulfillment. I am grateful for all of the decisions I have made so far and where they have led me. I am grateful for everything I have been given so far, have now, and that is yet to come.

When I look at where I have come from and where I am today, I can only say that it gives me more confidence for the future decisions I have to make. Even if these choices might be difficult and I can't see where they are going to take me, I trust that if my gut feeling says it's the right thing to do, then I should continue to push myself and ask "… And Why Not?"

Thoughts & Reflections

Chapter 4

TRUST THE PROCESS -
EVERYTHING WILL BE OKAY

We are often told to "trust the process," and believe me, I know that this is easier said than done. Especially when you are about to make a decision that will cause a significant change in your life. Especially when you don't know what will happen next. Especially when most of us are taught that we should not trust things blindly.

To clarify, I am not saying that you should trust whatever comes into your life blindly. In certain situations, this is obviously not a good idea. For example, we should not trust a perfect stranger in the street if we don't know what their intentions are. We have to take care of ourselves and not place ourselves or others in dangerous situations.

What I am saying is there is a process of evaluating a situation, weighing up the pros and cons, and making a conscious decision about what makes the most sense to you. And once you have made the decision and decided to follow your gut as it feels right to you, then let go and trust that your decision will take you to the right place.

Again, I know this is easier said than done for many people. Personally, I have always been someone who knows what she wants, has a plan, and knows where things are heading. But life put me to the test on this one big change I made. Yes, I had an idea of where it could all head, but suddenly, it was like I'd opened a door to infinite possibilities. Many times, I felt like I didn't know where to begin. Should I paint and make it a business? Should I write a book? Should I do a master's degree? Should I move forward with my boutique hotel project? And so on… I think you get the picture.

I sometimes wanted the answer right away so that I could get on with my project or whatever I decided to move forward with, but it wasn't as easy as that. So, I had to learn to trust the process. Trust that the decision I had made that had led me to this situation was the right decision and that I would figure all of it out at the right time.

Rather than focusing on figuring out this puzzle, which made my mind wheels spin at 1,000 miles per hour and led me nowhere, I had to let go. I had to trust and enjoy the process, remaining open and alert to opportunities. Then, things would fall into place at the perfect time. And perhaps the traced path of what I had in mind could be even better if I gave some leeway for other things that I hadn't envisioned in my plan.

Sometimes, we might think "I want to be rich so I'll buy a lottery ticket and realize my dreams!" I'm not saying you should not buy a lottery ticket as it is a way of getting rich. But perhaps life has a different plan for you, and you will get rich by developing a business or making an investment or inventing something, rather than just getting easy money. Perhaps you might think that winning the lottery would be the best option, but have you really thought of the consequences this can bring? Often, lottery winners end up back where they started, and sometimes even worse off. Along the way, they get into family conflicts, lose friends, and draw people into their life who are only there for a certain lifestyle, and when the person truly needs them, they disappear.

As mentioned earlier, I believe there is some sort of plan for each of us in the grand scheme of things, and we are all here to learn something specific to each of us. (Though this is just my view based on my own experience.)

My point is that when you're making a decision, ask yourself:
What is it that I am trying to achieve?
Where do I see myself a few years down the road?
Can the decision I am about to make take me there?

Perhaps you have a very clear idea or perhaps just a vague one.

Either way, try to visualize and see yourself in the situation you want to achieve. Or if it's not clear at all, try to feel the feeling you want to reach. Then, let go and trust that if you are meant to get there, life will put the right tools and opportunities across your path to get there. But also, be open that life may have other plans for you to reach an even better place than what you imagined, so learn to go with the flow.

Is this the famous "Power of Manifestation," you might be wondering? Perhaps. But if we have this opportunity to make choices in our life that enable us to realize our dreams and live a more fulfilled life, then ask yourself "… And Why Not?"

thoughts & Reflections

 Chapter 5

YOU ARE NOT ALONE

I consider myself very fortunate for the life I have lived up to now. I have been blessed with very supportive parents who have always encouraged me to do what I love and reach for the stars.

My family has been my pillar throughout my life. I could always come back to them to celebrate my successes but also get guidance and encouragement from them in times of doubt or when things didn't go as expected.

Likewise, my friends have always been there at the right time to chat, exchange experiences, or simply have a good time, so I could put aside my problems and come back to them later with a fresh mind.

But enough about me… My point is that even though people often say "You come to this world alone and leave it alone." That might be true from a scientific perspective, but you are not alone throughout your lifetime. Whether it's your family, friends, pets, or people who cross your path at one point in your life… you are not alone! There is always someone you can count on, whether for a season or a lifetime.

Of course, I know people who haven't been as fortunate

as me to grow up in a supportive family, and that might be the case for you, but that doesn't mean you are worse off or someone else is better off. It's just an opportunity to find those important people. As they say, "You might not choose your family but you can choose your friends." You can build your own support system. You have the power to decide who you want to let into your life.

It's important that you surround yourself with people who will be there for you in the good and the not-so-good times. Especially at the times when you have a situation that makes you re-question life and deliberate on your priorities. Especially when you feel a little lost. And especially when you feel like everyone seems to be telling you that the decision you are about to make is stupid, even though it feels right inside of you.

There will always be more than enough people trying to discourage you and judge your decisions, trying to dissuade you from pursuing what you have decided to pursue. Whether they are doing it purposely, as they don't want to see you surpass them, or unintentionally because they think they know best and want to protect you, there will always be people trying to hold you back.

If you can find or surround yourself with at least one person who is able to listen to you and come back to you from a completely neutral perspective, this is the best gift you can give yourself. These people don't necessarily give you their opinion or tell you what to do, but they ask you the right questions or use the right tools to help you uncover your own answers.

Yes, you might say "Well, that sounds like getting a consult from a psychologist!" And why not? Call them your guru, your friend, your coach, your psychologist, your family member, your mentor… it doesn't matter.

Have someone or a method, like meditation, bring you back to a point of neutrality. Trust me, when you reach that point of neutrality, you will know what decision to make. When you face a life-changing situation or are at a point in your life where you feel you need to shuffle things around, make a career change, or move environment, it can be quite an unsettling experience—especially as your emotions and ego get involved (and I can tell you, they will try to get in your way).

If you are able to put aside your fear, emotions, and ego and come back to what some refer to as "the neutral mind," you will see that the answer you were looking for has always been inside of you. But often, we need people, tools, or methods to help us get there.

You might be asking yourself "Why does she keep insisting on people? This is personal; it's my problem, and I can sort this on my own…" Yes, I get you. I used to think like that—I internalized many things until I came to a decision and sorted it out in my mind like a big girl. It's not impossible to do this yourself, but it can be an extremely energy-consuming exercise.

Sometimes, I did this out of fear of showing weakness and worrying about what people would think of me. So, I told myself "I will sort this on my own! This is silly. I must be the only one in this situation." Well, let me break it to you… there is no right or wrong way to do this but trust me when I say that sometimes, speaking to the right person can be an eye-opening experience.

You might say "But I don't like sharing my problems, and I don't like talking to people." That's fair enough. However, humans are by default social animals (albeit some more so than others). And so, sometimes, the exercise of speaking out and getting something off your chest can be such a relieving experience, even if you don't find your answer right away. A conversation with someone might just be the trigger point where you realize that the pressure you were feeling inside was blocking you from seeing the answer.

Sometimes, even going to a social or networking event that has nothing to do with what you're facing can make a difference. This can be a simple conversation of "What do you do for a living?" or "What are you up to these days?" Even sharing the least amount of detail, like "Well," I do this, and I'm currently questioning what I will do next…" can make a difference. Indeed, you might be surprised to realize that the person in front of you is going through the same thing.

All I want to say here is that even if you feel alone in your own world with your own problems, we are not individual humans but a community, and we share far more things in common with one another than you might think.

Thoughts & Reflections

Chapter 6

STAY OPEN

As they say, "If you don't ask, you won't get." It's as simple as that. If you want an answer or need help, and if you don't ask, you will never know. It might sound obvious, but it's good to be reminded every now and then. Many people, myself included, often end up forgetting that it's okay to ask for help.

When I speak about asking, I don't like to limit myself to a specific person but instead look at it from a broader, universal perspective. You can ask a person, yourself, the angels, saints, nature, or whatever your belief system is. You can simply throw a question out to life in general. You will always get an answer. Not necessarily the one you expected or the way you expected it, but if you stay open and alert, the answer will come to you.

Some people are more sensitive than others in being receptive to signs or getting answers to questions. Others need the answers to be a bit more explicit. Either way, whatever your question is, you will notice as time passes that the answer was always there for you.

It could be as simple as asking yourself the question "Should I go for it and attend an interview for a new job?" then suddenly in the street outside someone screams "Yes!" It might be you coming across a TV or social media advert where the message is "Take a chance." There are infinite ways in which you can get an answer to a question you are asking yourself, and life will find a way for you to get it. Perhaps you are a person who believes in the meaning of animals or flowers, then you ask a question and suddenly come across a beautiful flower or picture of an animal that makes it clear to you what life is trying to tell you.

I have come across people who are even more specific and say, for instance, "If I should move forward, show me a rainbow." This doesn't mean it's going to rain right away and suddenly out of nowhere, a rainbow will pop up. But perhaps in the next few days, you will come across an image that has a rainbow in it or are watching a movie where there is suddenly a scene of a rainbow or someone on the bus next to you is reading a book with "Rainbow" in the title. Again, what I am saying is ask your question, then let go and stay open to receiving the answer in some way.

I've tested this myself, and I'll share a simple example with you. I once took an exam, which I had studied and prepared for. When I came out of it, I knew I had done my best but there were a few questions I wasn't entirely sure I had answered correctly. I thought that this proportion of questions, even if incorrect, shouldn't jeopardize me passing the test, but you never know.

Rather than letting my mind drive me crazy for the weeks to come until the exam results were out, I decided to test the practice and asked "If I have passed the test, I will come across a bright orange flower."

I didn't get the answer right away, but I decided to go on with my daily life and stay open to a sign. Two days later, I was going grocery shopping and what did I see at the entrance of the store? A magnificent bouquet of bright orange flowers. A few weeks later, I received my test scores confirming that I had indeed passed the exam. Sure, you could say it was just a coincidence. Perhaps, but maybe not?

When it comes to staying open, it doesn't just apply to the types of answers you might get but also the opportunities that come your way. Again, you might have everything planned out in detail in terms of how you want and imagine things to occur. But perhaps there is a better way, and if you stay open to the opportunities that come your way in your decision path, perhaps you might take a slight detour or a slightly different direction that will get you to an even better place than what you imagined.

The universe is infinite, and so are the opportunities and ways of getting guidance and answers in life. Perhaps this book helps you get closer to the answer you are seeking at this stage of your life, or maybe it leads you to something else or another person or situation… I am a firm believer that there are no coincidences in life and there is an order to everything.

All I am saying is to stay open. You never know what might come your way… perhaps an opportunity or an answer you might not be expecting, but if it is meant to take you to a better place, then ask yourself "...And Why Not?"

Thoughts & Reflections

Chapter 7

THERE IS ALWAYS A REASON

It's probably not the first time you have heard this, and it's certainly not the last time, but there is always a reason for things. Whether the reason is clear from the start or you see it later, there is always a reason.

When your parents told you as a child to be careful and look both ways before crossing the road, there was obviously a reason behind it—they didn't want you to get hurt. However, there are also situations where the reason isn't that obvious to spot at the beginning, and what makes it difficult is that you somehow have to trust what is happening while you wait to reach the point where you can look back and say "Oh, now I get it!"

Let's take a look at a more concrete example. Perhaps you have decided to switch careers, which is already a big deal. You have gained the required certifications and done the relevant studies, but when you start applying for jobs in the new field, all you get is no for an answer.

You apply for months, and one day you get an interview for a position you really like the sound of. The interview process goes well, you get all the way to the last round of interviews, and it all looks very promising, so you start projecting and imagining yourself in this new job. Two weeks later, you find out that although you have an impressive CV, the company has decided to hire the other candidate. "Why?!" you might ask yourself.

Then, your mind starts spinning and planting doubts about yourself. You think perhaps you aren't good enough, and that it's tougher than you expected it to be, and that you're never going to make it, and that you probably made the wrong choice to leave your old career…

STOP!!!

Don't let your head get wrapped up in all of this. If you start going down this path, just give your mind and yourself the command to "Stop!"

You, yes you, are more than worthy. You are as capable as anyone else of achieving your dreams. And you had the courage to make a change to reach a better place in life. Trust yourself and trust that if you've made the right choice— because your gut told you so—you will get there. Again, it's easier said than done, but all I can say is persevere and be patient. When the time is right, the right opportunity will come.

Going back to the example of not getting your dream job… you could ask yourself "Was it really my dream job or a job that would enable me to thrive, be happy, and do what I love?" Perhaps at that very moment, your answer might be yes. Yet, a few months down the line, you get a call or are contacted by an old acquaintance who invites you for a coffee to catch up, which changes things. As you are chatting with them and telling them about your journey, they suddenly say that you are the person they have been looking for and they have a proposition for you to join a project that enables you to do what you love and have 10 times more freedom than the other job you had applied for.

Well? If the first company hadn't closed the door, you probably would have missed out on this amazing opportunity. So now you understand why the other company said no. Or at least you are now in a position to grasp an even better opportunity being presented to you.

I am not saying it's easy because it's not, especially if you are the type of person who likes to see where things are going and plan accordingly. Especially if you are in a situation where you feel a bit lost and have people telling you "Trust that when the time is right, you will get the answer or find what you need," it may get you more frustrated. You want the right time to be now or to find a crystal ball and see what awaits you, so at least you know! And rather than enjoying the moment and trusting the process, you feel anguish and stress because it's a very uncomfortable situation to be in.

Well, if life has decided that you need to learn patience, it will teach you this! And until you let go and decide to trust and be patient, things will not unfold for you. So, at the end of the day, you think that life is imposing this on you but actually, you are the one holding the door and stopping it from opening.

Yes, I may sound annoying but let me call upon my experience and confirm to you that it's worth the wait.

There is a reason for everything, and if you remain open and stick to the choice you have made, you will be surprised by the wonderful things life has reserved for you… even if you have to be a bit patient and wait to see the results.

If you know there is a reason for what you are going through and it's just a matter of time before you receive a wonderful gift, then what is there to lose? If you will be in a place ten times better than you can imagine right now, ask yourself "...And Why Not?"

Thoughts & Reflections

Chapter 8

you know
?

AND WHY NOT?

So here we are, at the concluding chapter of this book. A relatively short and sweet book, but if you can get your message across clearly (and hopefully I have) without having to explain yourself in 1,000 pages, then why not?

The most important thing for me is that after reading these pages, you have hopefully been able to find something that will guide you in the right direction or perhaps bring you the comfort you needed at this stage of your journey. Or you've simply found a different take on life—one that will give you the courage to follow your gut and bring the change into your life you need to make.

I am no scientist or philosopher, but I am a human being who carries the expertise of my own life and would find it sad if I were to keep my own experiences and learned lessons to myself. It is my conviction that if you can share something, even if just a single word or gesture, and it can make a difference in someone else's life, then it is totally worth it.

You have the power to change and make a change in your life. Never underestimate yourself, nor let someone make you believe you are not able to do it. You are the only one who can set your own limits, so if you want to go further than your limits, unlock the door that stops you from going beyond them and achieving your dreams.

If it feels right deep inside of you, then go for it! There is nothing worse than living with regrets.

You want to be an artist? Or a baker? A coach? Change your career? Travel the world? If that's what feels right deep inside of you, then who is there to stop you but yourself?

At some point in our lives, we all go through change, and I believe that we all come across similar questions or situations. However, many people facing a fork in the road of their lives often feel that the whole weight of the world is upon them and that the situation they are in is unique and insurmountable. Well, let me reassure you that the mere fact of me writing these pages shows that you are not alone.

You have the right to strive to live a more fulfilled life, and even though the journey might not be easy and you might be faced with tough choices, if your gut is telling you it's the right move to make, then stay open and embrace the change. If you have the slightest doubt before taking that step, then ask yourself "...And Why Not?"

Here is my last gift to you before this book ends, which I encourage you to read and remind yourself of every day...

You are beautiful

You are smart

You are courageous

You are loved

You can make a change

WHAT'S NEXT?

If you would like to see more of my artistic work and creations, you can follow me on Instagram @sm_art_paintings

ACKNOWLEDGMENTS

This book would not be possible without my editor Ameesha Green and her wonderful team, The Book Shelf Ltd, who guided and advised me all the way through the publishing process.

www.ingramcontent.com/pod-product-compliance
Lightning Source LLC
LaVergne TN
LVHW051507180726
843512LV00006B/689